THE SONG

Calvin Miller

InterVarsity Press
Downers Grove
Illinois 60515

© 1977 by Inter-Varsity Christian Fellowship of the United States
of America.

InterVarsity Press is the book-publishing division of Inter-Varsity
Christian Fellowship, a student movement active on campus at hundreds
of universities, colleges and schools of nursing. For information
about local and regional activities, write IVCF, 233 Langdon St., Madison,
WI 53703.

Distributed in Canada through InterVarsity Press, 1875 Leslie St.,
Unit 10, Don Mills, Ontario M3B 2M5, Canada.

ISBN 0-87784-785-1

Library of Congress Catalog Card Number: 77-74843

Printed in the United States of America

19	18	17	16	15	14	13	12	11	10	9	8	7
91	90	89	88	87	86	85	84	83	82	81	80	

1

In the middle of the faithless
sky there hangs a small, dark
world that once was green and
blue.

Some say it killed itself by
stabbing all its lovely lands
with deep atomic wounds.
Some say it took an overdose
of hate.

When words are rare as gems,
then sentences are mined at
great expense. In such a time
the tiny planet Terra swung
its mindless orbits in constant
hunger for a word that would
not come. Silence stalked the
universe and Earthmaker would
not speak. There was little
that his love could say to
a vicious world so fond of
tearing holes in his beloved.

It was agreed by common guilt
that spirit had turned its back
on matter. Earthmaker had set
his face away from the place of
execution and was staring outward
toward glittering and unspoiled
star-fields. For Terra was a field
of tombs—a universal junkyard where
his creatures quarreled for refuse
and waged great wars over who
should own the wreckage of their times.

Messiahs were abundant, but all
of them were egotists who hawked
joy-plated creeds through their
fading empires.

The men of Terra made a dull
discovery in the tepid days
that closed upon the Singer's
disappearance: When Earthmaker
will not speak to men, they have
nothing of importance to say to
each other.

11

There is but one good illustration
of SPIRIT—WIND!
Everything else is too visible.

When Spirit comes to flesh
gales rage and zephyrs scream.
When he withdraws, air
stagnates and insects
build webs in the rotors
of the silent mills.

The Madman spoke only words
that would not wait—
the small and mindless things
it took to keep life at a
distance great enough
to breathe.

The thick, hot air clotted commerce
and forced all men to wade its deadness.
The desert leered at villagers
and waited with the condors for
life to change to carrion.

The Madman took his turn in the line
at the village well. Like all the
rest he held a bucket which he hoped
to fill. Everyone in line still nursed
the fear that the ancient well
would fail. When it did, the
town would die. Each man hoped for
rain and begged the question:
"When comes the wind?"

The Madman felt the final hint of
moving air the day the Singer left—
the day the sun moved closer and
the breezes stopped. Half-truths
had festered in the lifeless air,
for most believed The Lie which
taught the Singer had died that
shrouded night the timbers
tumbled to the ground.

Rumors raged. Doubt was universal
for the scholars agreed that no
one could live through the cursed

ordeal of the machine, much less
its fall from ancient battlements.

There were some who said the
drought that fell upon the world
was the vengeance of the mountain
gods angered at the cruelty of
"holy men" who murdered only when
they wore the sacred garb of priests.
Some said it thundered twice each
day at the precise and awful moment
that they broke his hands. Yet
it never thundered on the plains
—only in the highlands.

The sun kept shorter nights and
walked a slower arch across the
cloudless skies. The dry earth
cracked its wrinkled, powdered
crust. The well rope grew dry
further down its braided coil,
and the water-bearers fell at
midday under shaded eaves.

III

What do you have, young prophet
   bold?
Some new, wide dream of scope?
Written by fire in the snowy cold
On silver plates of hope?

I found him under a tree grown old
And hanged with a doctrine rope.
Some said he thought the tree was
   young.

On the first day of the month of
Krios an old woman came from the
mountains and, bent above her gnarled
stick, she made her way from door
to door. She sang in feeble syllables
the song the Grand Musician once
had sung before official executioners.
She bore a weathered scroll beneath
her tattered sleeve and sang her
tuneless, toneless, tasteless dirge.

She was deaf but quite devoted,
committed to the creed she sang
aloud but had not heard in years.

They asked her if the wind blew in
the mountains. She could not hear,
but the musty odor made it clear
no breeze had blown on her.
Her scroll had not been ruffled by
the mountain wind nor moistened by
the rain. The dust upon the ragged
roll had not been stirred to rise
or settle back again.

While she stood in line before the well,
she died. She did not fall. She only
stared in death as she had stared in life.
And no one seemed to know the
instant of her passing. The
village sexton found her hard
to bury. Her passing seemed a
little matter. No one mourned.

The first of Krios passed.
And on the second of the month
the Madman prayed again,

"Earthmaker, Father of the Singer,
send us now the ancient wind
of promise." He knew the wind
he craved would bring the rain.

He knew that Terra's lover was also
the Keeper of the Winds. And while
he could not know the exact galactic
place, he knew the great Father-Spirit
sat starward in the breeding place
of suns. His light-blazed dais
was founded on the filaments of
constellations never seen on Terra.
And there where all the universal
light converged, and slightly to the
right, stood erect the object of all
universal joy—the Singer, who waited
for Earthmaker to send him back again
into the world that they both loved.

As the planet measured time, the
time was near. The third of Krios
stood just a dawn away. And when
it came, the Court of Ages Gone
would wait in rapt salute until
the Singer folded all his singing
soul into the gracious wind. And
then the raging gales would leave the
splendor of foreverness and break
in hurricanes of love upon the
thirsty world.

The Madman rose from prayer and
walked at noon toward the well.
In the burning way he met a man
who bore a shovel and a scroll.

"Good day, Sexton!" he called.
"You feel compelled to bury
scrolls?"

"No, Madman, I took it from the old
woman who died in the water line,"
the sexton answered. "Old women
should be buried, but never books.
Do you read?"

"I read," the Madman said.

"Then here," said the sexton as he
handed him the woman's one possession.

The Madman took the roll and stared
in fascination at its crinkled skin.
"The book is old," he thought.
"She must have started writing
it when she was very young."

He waited for his measure of water
and then he left the well. He en-
tered his barren room and waited
in the shuttered silence for the
dusk. He ate a crust of bread and
drank a little water. The water,
like the earth, was dead. Nothing
sparkled on the tongue. When darkness
came, he lit an oil wick and broke
the heavy seal upon the scroll. It
opened to the very place of promise
and the ancient words stared up at him.

"The writer was the woman, prior to her
blindness," he said into the gloom.

She had indeed written all the scroll,
this strange old Amazon, whose stories
coursed with dragons and winged
creatures she had seen. Sometimes she
wrote of armies, their conflict set
in blood. And then again she told of
shepherds singing songs and maidens deep

in love with unremembered sheiks.
Sometimes she wrote the mindless,
droning genealogies of her glorious
heritage. Law was there.
Love was there.
Life, justice, death.

The lamp burned low before his eyes
fell on the Song of Promise. The
text came up in joy and hung about
him, robed in the simple glory of
its years:

"O clap your hands
    you dying heads of state!
His love will come to cleanse
    the practiced hate
    of fallen Terra.
Joy will come again
    to fill the deserts,
    level mountain chains.

Earthmaker is in love
    with loveless men.
The God of Storms and Keeper
    of the Winds will come.
The Father-Spirit's only Troubadour
    reserves the heavy gales
    behind the door of Life.
Cry out remorse for hate and sin.
Life comes for all,
    astride the Singing Wind."

IV

An old woman buried three sons.
At the funeral of the first she was
a cynic.
At the funeral of the second she
called herself a seeker.
At the third... a weeping
believer.

By evening, those who waited for
the wind did so in despair. Gaunt
and face to face with death, they knew
the dying was not hard; the burning
journey into death would be. The
children whimpered for the bread
and water that soon would cease.

Some blamed the Father-Spirit.
Some did not.

The yellow earth like dry rot stole
the hope of day and caused old men
to pull their leprous rags about
their ochre faces and spit into the
jaundiced sky and curse Earthmaker.

A mother of twins stood waiting
while the dry well rope uncoiled
from around the crank. She heard
the clatter of the empty bucket
on the rocks below . . . The
rope began to wrap itself around
the windlass once again. When it
reached the top, the bucket and
the rope were dry. So were the men
of Terra, for the time they feared
had come.

In hopeless hope the rope was once
more lowered in the well. Again
the bucket came up dry. Anger
swelled and a temper-ridden man
strode to the well and grabbed
the sexton by his coat. He raised
his voice indignantly and cursed
the sexton for the failure of the well.

His babbled threats were sounds
that never would make words.
The sexton, paralyzed, struggled hard
to understand; he tried to speak
to his assailant, but his earnestness
was also lost in strange new sounds.
Another man came from the crowd to
arbitrate and though his sounds were
syllables of peace he too could form
no words.

Fear came upon the city. Words,
like water, ceased to be. Paragraphs
of gibberish proceeded, but not com-
munication. Wails without words rose
from the yellow dust.

Anxiety closed in with night.
A wordless mass hysteria became the
common dread that each one knew but
none could speak. And when words
die, the little fears become the
terrors of the night. They knew
that death would come and when
it did all men would die without
a cry of hope or sensible despair.
No final statements and no eulogies
—no reaching out for touch. Life
would die together—all, at once,
yet separately. And none could
even say "Good-bye!"

Terra kills, but Terra will not die.
Heartless Terra will not even
Let her children cry.
Terra is a spinning vault,
A mass of dusty graves,
The tombyard of her dreamers,
The mausoleum of her brave.

Terra has just one stone
To mark her great insanity:
Across her continents it reads:
"HERE LIES HUMANITY!"

V

Death is a crone
who grins only when the pulse
is weak, and smiles only in
full when breathing stops.
She grasps her dying
globe and smiles—
a grim madonna gloating on her
sickly child.

As the wail rose in the streets,
Sarkon, the World Hater, smiled at
a triumph which he knew would be
short-lived. He braced himself
for what he saw ahead. He had
decided to become the herald of
the mountain gods, though all the
mountain gods were dead.

He hated Terra as he always had.
He gloated on her exile, pleased
that her disease was terminal.
Like other aging planets, she would
die. But well he knew her time of
dying was not yet. She would recover
from the current illness in her streets
and die when men were more intelligent—
less wise.

In the meantime he would try
to draw men from Earthmaker. He
would need a trick or two and
for his purposes non-existent gods
would do.

Sarkon liked the mountain gods
for they were made in man's own
image. He knew what mortals never
seemed to learn: The more the gods
become like men, the easier it is
for men to believe the gods. When
both have only human appetites, then
rogues may worship rogues.

Meanwhile he enjoyed seeing
Terra at the point of death. He
smiled because her desperation was

intense. He made his way through
the streets to the quarters of a
man he had met a thousand times
before, but when he reached the
Madman's door, a sheet of fire
blocked his way.

Inside, the great Earthmaker drew
a soft embrace around his lonely
child, who sought to pray the sick-
ness from the streets.

"It is good to be your child,
Earthmaker," the Madman said aloud.

"It is good to own you," said
the darkness with impressive
silence. "Madman, you are sane—
more sane than any dweller on this
orb. You may no longer wear a
name that lies. From now you will
be Anthem, for you will be the
Herald of the Anointing. The
power of Earthmaker will be yours,
to bear the Singer and his Song
before the kings of Terra."

Then Anthem fondled his new name,
and turned it over in his heart.
Tomorrow he would take his name
and enter a new age. Tomorrow he
would come and bring with him the
promised Age of Gold. His name was
quite as eloquent as that great flame
that kept his gate. The fiery wall
left Sarkon a vagabond to walk alone
in hate.

VI

It takes a breeze
to make a banner speak.

The third of Krios wrapped itself
in gray. The sun was merciful and
never rose. The morning brought a
breeze that stiffened to a gale. The
welcome smell of sweet young rain
became a furied hint of promises the
heavens shortly kept. Rain drenched
the earth in torrents of the love
that great Father-Spirit now scattered
in the dust.

So Terra came alive and people ran
into the streets to feel the water
and the wind. None were ashamed
to see themselves soaked in driving,
blinding rain.

It was the changing of the age—
the great fulfillment of the ancient
vow the woman wrote down in her
scroll. And as the rain streamed
down his face, Anthem also praised
Earthmaker that his Beloved had come
back. He stood and shouted out
above the crowd:
"Earthmaker rides the Wind.
The Singer has returned..."

Silence roared.
Sound ripped through density.
Communication coursed again
through human isolation. And
Anthem spoke—no longer gibberish—
but words and sentences, and all his
words were understood.

"How is it," cried the crowd,
"that we now hear with understanding
and the gift of words is given?"

When Anthem raised his hand and
called the wild excitement to a
calm, the wind made way for words.
His Wind Song then began.

"The Eagle has returned.
    The shattered sky
Has fallen back. And Terra's
    victory
Is sure. The Singer whom we
    caused to die
Has come to slay time
    with infinity.

The Father-Spirit and his
    Troubadour
Have brought the Great Invader
    and his Age
Of Gold. For they were old
    when nature tore
Away the vacuum at its heart.
    Love raged.

And then the trebled Spirit
    mystery
Was one. Yet love begun
    in open space
Would swell in joy till
    one was three—
His factor of infinity
    in grace.

And never shall his Terra
    understand
This cosmic riddle born
    ahead of men;

How Spirit can become
    a sinewed hand
And then a cosmic Spirit
    once again.

Never was it one but
    always three.
Never was it three but
    always one.
Claiming boldly it would
    always be—
Yet crying out it never
    had begun.

Let men embrace the rain.
    Come, Wind, blow free
And stir the warm sweet breeze!
    Dream, dreamless men!
Our empty youth come filled
    with prophecy.
Our grunts now Spirit-washed
    are words again.

The Great Invader breathes upon you
    as a man
Of Holy Fire, from that far land
    where all
Horizons meet. He knocks
    with wounded hands
Upon the soul. And penetrates
    the wall

Of your resistance to Earthmaker's
    love.
The Spirit of the Singer
    comes to sing
An inner melody.
    To fill above
Our brim of joy his own
    abundant being.

Weep, Terra! For yours is
    the ugly crime
That killed the Song and struck
    Earthmaker dumb.
You stabbed eternal life
    with dismal time
And murdered him who was and
    is to come.

O men of Terra! Ours is
    the shame,
Of standing heavy-footed
    on his name.
Beside the star-blazed dais
    there he stands.
We clawed the face of love then
    broke his hands.

Cry out! O men, cry out! The blood
    we spilt
Has left us refugees from love.
    And sin
Has left us in a wilderness
    of guilt.
Trust in the joy that swims
    Invader's Wind."

And then the rain drew back, and eerie
light converged upon the rain-soaked
streets. A column of brightness
gathered itself from the gleam of
cobblestones and fled in a fiery instant
into the sky.

And at the top a mystic beam of majesty
tumbled down in music. A chord then
turned to thunder that shook the earth.
Earthmaker so blazed in radiance
that men cried out in fear and love
at once.

The dazzling hurricane of light
fell full on Terra's shame
and a fiery brilliant radiance
proclaimed his mighty name—
Invader.

VII

Where do the old gods live?

　In temples tended by old, old men.

And the young gods?

　In young men who dream

　of building temples so that they

　will have something to tend when

　they are old, old men.

It is better to believe than dream.

For dreams grow old and so do

　dreamers.

Dreamers die but not believers.

An old man lifted up his face and
wept before the transfixed crowd.
He called out through his tears,
"What must I do to be unchained?"

And Anthem answered, "Admit your
emptiness. Open to the Wind.
Receive the Stigmon of the Singer."

"I will. Come in, Invader," he
cried into the swirling radiance.
He held his leathered face in
wrinkled hands, and when he
took his hands away, he wore a
strange new countenance of light.

Anthem reached down and scooped
a handful of moist earth.
"Do you believe the Singer is
alive and that he is Earthmaker's Son?"

"Yes," cried the old man in a husky
voice, choked by the fullness of
his joy.

"Then," said Anthem, "receive the
Stigmon." He traced upon the old man's
face the Singer's Sign with earth
and spoke:
"It is only out of Terra's shame
That men of Terra wear the name
Of Singer,
Prince of Planets,
Troubadour of Life."

And then he placed a small amount
of the remaining soil in the old

man's hand, as he breathed the last
lines of the Stigmon:
"Remember as your hand is stained
That his was crushed and torn by pain
That men of Terra fully know
There is no depth he would not go
To Love.
Earthmaker, Singer and Invader be
The substance of infinity."

The old man suddenly found himself in a
sea of thirsty faces crying out to the
Invader to enter them in the storm of
light that now enveloped all.

Hundreds were invaded and the Singer
added to this number all who were un-
chained and had received the Stigmon.
Their foreheads were smudged with
the Singer's Sign and their hands bore
the symbol of his wounds.

The day was long and lovely and
substance slept with a thousand hearts
by fall of night. It was the dawning
of the Age of the Invader.

VIII

The fable reminds us:

A witch may beguile us with apples!

Beware old women selling green fruit.
Their sales deceive.

Who spares a witch may but
   a serpent save.
A dying dragon digs a witch's grave.
We seldom trust the fairy tales
Until we gasp in claws and scales.

Anthem slept a lovely sleep that
would have lasted through the night
except the fire before his gate
was gone. So in the center of
the night he was awakened by the
rapping of an old familiar hand
outside his room. He lit the lamp
and opened up the door. His faint
light fell into the night before
the fingers of the dark pinched
out the amber fire.

Seeing no one, he closed the door, then
bolted it in fear. And sitting on his
bed he called into the dark, "Hater,
give back my flame." The darkness
would not answer him, till in a firmer
voice he almost shouted,
"I now command you in the
Singer's name and the name of his
machine of death, give back my light
and then give substance to yourself."

Instantly the lamp relit itself.
Its light fell out upon a handsome
youth.

"Are you unchained?" the young man
asked.

"Yes," Anthem said. He tried to
match the fairness of the youth
with what he thought that he would
see. "I want all the light you took
from me, World Hater!"

The flame burned brighter still.

"Yes, I'm unchained—invaded, too."
Then Anthem spoke in boldness, "I
know you are the World Hater in
disguise. And I no longer fear the
pipe you play that once drove me
insane."

"I gave my pipe away, Madman..."
His voice trailed off in huskiness.

"My name is not Madman, it is
Anthem. The Father-Spirit says I
am too sane to wear the name you
gave me, Hater."

"Please... do not call me World
Hater now—my name is Sarkon."

"You do still hate the world?"

The boy then smirked. The tendons
rippled in his ivory neck. He drew
a slur across his heavy lips. "Of
course I hate. But Terra will not
know. Every one will see Sarkon
a lover whose affection is much
stronger than the love of..."
His mouth still moved but would not
frame the word.

"You cannot say 'The Singer' can you?
Your hate has no coordination
for such a lovely name."

"Yes," the youth went on, "I, Sarkon,
will pose as Terra's lover, try to
pry her from her track and roll her
into some galactic hole filled with
stellar putrefaction. I am committed
to her last destruction. I have

infected every corner with the desire
for power and greed, as you will see.
I have smeared the continents with
lust for blood not even your Invader
can swab clean."

"A thousand were unchained today,"
said Anthem.

"But millions still are mine and
hate the myth you love."

"It isn't myth, Hater!"

"I've told you that my name is
Sarkon now. Do you notice
any newer facets to my form,
Anthem?"

"You're taller somehow. Studied,
handsome, muscular. Your hair looks
like a sculptured head I once saw in
a pagan shrine. You look much like
a mountain god."

Sarkon was delighted. "I am—
fresh from a temple men can see.
Yes, I am man as he was meant to
be—ideal humanity—managerial and
strong, empirical and wise
with answers that are more visible
than yours. And I know science
too. Come talk with me about
creation and you will be embarrassed
by my questions."

Anthem grew angry. "I thought
you said you would have answers
from your sciences and now you
talk of questions."

"I've answers to your answers;
and questions for your questions."

"And will men follow you for
only questions?"

"Of course they will, for nothing
else will have esteem. Your myths
grow weak when sciences grow strong.
I shall expose you, Anthem—you will
see. I'll ask you in the crowded
market place just how it is that
science is defied by all your magic
claims that executed Singers come
to life again."

When Sarkon stood, he truly seemed
the ideal man, a standard towards
which all men would strive,
what every man would want to be, at
least the ones content with merely
being men.

Then Sarkon snapped his fingers and
called out, "Old Woman, come at once
and stand again alive . . ."

And Anthem shuddered as he felt his
neck hair bristle. It was
incredible, but standing there beside
the rugged youth was the old woman
who had died before the city well.

"She is dead," stammered Anthem.
"The sexton buried her and I now
have her scroll."

"No, Anthem. Look! She's alive
just as you claim your Great Lover
is alive."

"I see a replica and that is all..."

Anthem stopped his speaking, and
looking up he called for more
authority than he alone possessed.
"Earthmaker, Father of the Singer,
remove the woman's mask and
let us see what treachery this is."

The woman groaned and stumbled to
her knees. At once a hideous strength
fell scaled upon the floor and slithered
over Sarkon's feet. Its green-brown
gills croaked out a strange defiance of
the presence in the life of Anthem.

"Sarkon," he said, "it was nothing
but a trick. It was only a dragon
that you feed in your great pit."

"Perhaps," replied the youth. "But
some who do not know the Singer will
believe this monster is the author
of the scroll you have. Between this
woman and myself will lie a path of
blood for you. You cannot win,
poor Anthem."

"Take your ugly pet and go," he
cried. They left in fiendish laughter
that rattled windows and vanished
in the air.

Then peace acquired the place that
conflict had so lately held, and
stayed the night. Anthem slept.

But Sarkon waited for a student
whose troubled mind and heart had never
met. Sarkon vowed they never would.

IX

Science can change the
compound states of matter
easier than it can change
its mind.

The student known as Everyman was
indeed a troubled youth but grateful for
the wind and rain. Though he often
hungered to be free, he was not among
the thousand who had been unchained.

He accepted all the sciences as truth
but rejected all ideas that Earthmaker
could exist. Yet he sometimes wished
such mystic falsehoods true. For
those who claimed to be unchained seemed
so naive to Everyman. And yet they
seemed to own contentment he had never
managed in pursuing all his sciences.
He could not make himself believe
the Singer was the Father-Spirit's Son.
Nor did he trust the rumor that
the Singer had returned to life.
Yet the Singer haunted all his
idle hours.

Everyman's great appetites were
of the heart. He tried to sate his
hunger by devouring the philosophies
and sciences he loved. He read
the poems of the priests and mountain
gods, but their verses seemed as rigid
as the columns of their temples.

He read the woman's scroll, but
rejected all her rules and altar
laws. And now in the upheaval that
spread outward from the city's walls,
men everywhere rejoiced that the
Singer had returned, and that the
Golden Age had come.

Everyman was reading from a scroll
called the REASON OF EMPTINESS while
he lay on a grassy slope of summer.

"Hello!" called out a voice from
somewhere behind him. "What do
you read?"

Everyman looked up and then looked
back upon his book. He said,
"I read of reason."

"What reason?" queried the approach-
ing youth.

"The reason that teaches Terra made
herself when there were civil wars
among the stars."

"And do you think it true?" the
stranger asked when finally he
reached his side a little out of
breath.

"How can I tell?... Come now...
let us not begin with our philosophies
but with our names... I am Everyman."

"And I am Sarkon!"

"And tell me, Sarkon, do you believe?"

"Yes," said the handsome youth. "I
believe in all I am and nothing else.
I believe in eating when I hunger,
loving when I lust and sleeping when
I weary of the game."

"But of the current madness that

the Father-Spirit has a living
Son who sings?"

Sarkon laughed. "It's a myth
for ignorance to feed upon. You surely
do not seek to be unchained?"
he asked sarcastically.

"A thousand were, they say, upon
the third of Krios, when the Wind
blew."

"And do you think that you should
feel guilty just because the
Singer died?" asked Sarkon.

"No, of course I don't.
It's just..."

"What?"

"Well, those unchained seem filled
with what I lack somehow."

"They are," replied Sarkon. "They
all are filled with madness! Be
grateful that you lack what they
are filled with."

"Perhaps," said Everyman, staring
vacantly into the distant sky.
"Do you believe the Singer came
alive again?"

"No—not at all. I know the man
who buried him, you see. His grave
is in a country field..."

"Then let us go and dig him out

and show the unchained men of Terra
their great folly and absurdity."

Sarkon blushed. "I ... wh ..."
He stammered much before he finally
spoke. "The grave, I must regret,
lies far away. We have not time enough
to travel there today," he finally
explained. He quickly changed
the subject. "It's just as well,
believe me. Could you, good scientist,
believe that Terra was created when
the Singer sang in open space
and let all matter out of nothingness?"

"No, no. I'll trust the scholars
there. The Singer did not sing to
make the trees. Trees gathered up
their being from the seas. I know
that when we get the gods involved
no scientific issues are resolved.
But then why do I hunger for
more than I am fed from all the
scrolls of science?"

"You hunger," Sarkon said, "for
something else. Come, let us fill
our bellies so our minds will not
be restless, nor our hearts. I
know women who can make philosophy
an elementary matter. When lust has
eaten at the table of desire, you
will be satisfied again. When
the flesh feeds itself, the hunger
of the spirit is forgotten."

Sarkon stood. He was quite practical
it seemed to Everyman, who was tired
of study. Everyman also thirsted for
the taverns of the city where he and

Sarkon could forget their emptiness
of soul.

Everyman then stood, and as
he stood he said, "Let's go and
worship at the temple of indulgence
till all our appetites are full..."
And then he added, "Tomorrow, Sarkon,
could you take me to the man you spoke
about—the man who laid the
Singer in his grave?"

Sarkon looked away and paused, but
finally he said, "Tomorrow, I will
take you there."

X

At stonings angels stand apart
And weep above the martyrs' groans.
But demons always grin, and keep
Both hands grasping—filled with
  stones.

As Sarkon and Everyman came through
the city gates a street minstrel was
singing to a crowd. Sarkon despised
the poor who listened to the balladeer.

"Do you know the man who sings?"
asked Everyman.

"His name is Anthem," answered
Sarkon with no apparent interest.

"Isn't he the street singer who
sang the day the wind came from
the mountain?"

"He is. But careful, friend, or he
will have your science in his pouch.
You'll be dancing to his tunes."

They passed so near the street singer
they could hear the verses of his
song.

"Come to the Singer you science-stained.
Cry for the crime and be unchained
Here in the great Invader's reign."
The people who watched him as he
sang joined him in his simple melody.

Sarkon reached down and found
a heavy stone and hurled it.

The rock struck Anthem's forehead
such a blow he almost fell unconscious.
The song abruptly stopped. The little
group of street balladeers closed around
him as a shield.

Everyman, incensed by Sarkon,
turned on him and shouted:
"Why did you do that?"

"He sings a lie," said Sarkon.

"But still he is a man... Have you
some grudge that makes you hate him?
Are there reasons other than his song?"

"None. Come, the tavern is a better
place to talk," said Sarkon.

As they were leaving, Anthem was
revived, and Everyman could hear him
singing once again:
"Come, Terra. Let us sing of love
And the broken hand in the ragged glove.
For ours it is to be set free,
Unchained and given destiny."

"How can he sing?" thought Everyman.
He wanted to turn back, but he placed
his hand on the latch to the tavern door.

XI

Love is substance. Lust, illusion.
Only in the surge of passion
Do they mingle in confusion.

Dawn came swiftly on the eve of lust. When Everyman awoke his head was on the bosom of a maid.

"Did I satisfy you, Everyman?" she asked.

"Last night you did," he answered. "But now I hunger once again."

"For food or love or books?" she asked in deep sincerity.

"For none of these. For something more, if something more there be." And then he asked, "Where is my young and god-like friend? Still with his maid?"

"Which maid? Five went to him last night. His science is his appetite— ever eating, never full."

"Did he say that?" asked Everyman in disbelief.

"Oh no," the maid replied. "The thought was mine. He is a handsome rogue, but every night he prowls the taverns of the street and preys upon such souls as he may meet. Few tell him no. It's strange. Few like him, though none resist him long. He never drinks or sleeps alone ... Do you like him, Everyman?"

"Well, no. I guess not," he said, "though I never thought of it till

now. Tell me, maid, do you know a
balladeer named Anthem?"

"The crazy man, who sings to rabble
in the streets?"

"You know him then?
Where does he live?"

"Why, right above this tavern,"
she replied.

XII

Appetites ignored revolt
and break the windows of the
shops to get at food.
But hunger of the soul
grows weak with malnutrition
and begs a crust
of spirit.

The steps that waited on the upper room were old and rickety. But Everyman ascended them . . . hesitated . . . and knocked.

"Come in," said Anthem as he opened wide the door. "Are you not Sarkon's friend?" he asked.

"As he has friends," he said and then went on. "I cannot tell you why I've come, and yet I feel those who threw their stones at you were evil men."

The new scar glistened even in the scanty light of Anthem's room. "Sarkon's an ugly man and capable of ugly deeds."

Everyman was puzzled. "I thought Singerians never criticized another man."

Anthem could not bring himself to share with Everyman the truth. He knew the young man could not believe it all so soon.

"You did not come to dress my wound or tell me you were sorry for the injury."

"No, I have come because I've gorged and baptized every appetite in full indulgence and I am hungry still," said Everyman.

"Earthmaker has a living Son who fills all emptiness above the brim."

"So I have heard, yet I have
evidence—the Singer is a fraud.
Tonight the riddle will be solved,
for I will meet the man who laid
your Singer in the grave. He
put his mangled body in the ground
the night the great machine fell
off the wall and nothing has dis-
turbed his grave..."

"Did Sarkon promise you the
introduction?" Anthem asked.

"He did, in fact," Everyman replied.
"The digger of the Singer's grave
is his close friend."

Anthem was puzzled by the proposition.
What was Sarkon's hope in using such
a falsehood? He walked to a table piled
high with scrolls and scratched some
hasty words on a piece of parchment.

"Here, when you meet the digger of
the Singer's grave, open this folded
scrap of paper and read aloud the
words. But do not open it or read
it till then."

"I do not understand."

"You may quite soon," said
Anthem. They left the room together
and stepped into the streets.
Anthem began to sing.

And Everyman went back to the
fields to study science and hope
Sarkon would come by early afternoon.
He was not disappointed.

XIII

A magician pulls
bunnies out of empty hats.
An Evil Lord pulls reptiles
out of dank and crawling pits and
places writhing, muddy serpents
in the cradles of the infant saints.

When Sarkon appeared, he
was naked to the waist. The muscles
of his shoulders glinted bronze
beneath his strong neck and bold
head. He bore a discus with the
arrogance of self-assurance.

"Sarkon!" Everyman exclaimed.
"You are a god indeed!"

"Ah, ah, ah," the handsome youth
responded. "The gods are dead,
remember? Now there is only
science and yearning appetite.
How did you find your maid last
night?"

Everyman looked down. "I only
loved her while I lusted, and then
I hated her for making me recall
I am never satisfied for long."

"What are you reading from your
sciences today?" the churlish
Sarkon probed.

"Today I'm reading the scroll called
THE REASON OF SUBSTANCE. Did you
know that this small stone I prop
my foot against is a seething mass
of whirling orbs, each with its tiny
lightning storms and milky ways?"

"So I have heard, Everyman. And
are the tavern maids composed of
such minutiae—of dancing, shooting
particles of stars—of spinning

microworlds tearing orbits in the
center of their bosoms, and fleet-
ing beams of small galactic storms?"

"You've read the scrolls of science!"
said Everyman in glee.

"Enough to know that we are but a
gathering of microsuns, fast
moving asteroids that whirl at
lightning speed. But evening's
soon and we must get to the
taverns once again."

"Before we go, you promised me an
introduction," Everyman reminded
him.

"I did?"

"Yes. You said that I might meet the
man who laid the Singer in his grave."

"Oh yes... him." Sarkon grimaced
and then with added certainty he
acquiesced, "Very well, young scientist.
You shall meet the man indeed. He's
buried many singers I can tell you,
friend. His shovel never rusts.
Come right this way."

Everyman still marveled at the handsome
Sarkon, looking yet as though some
sorceress had blessed a statue in the
temple and set it free to tread the
planet and give the gaping men of Terra
an exhibition of divinity. Then
Everyman remembered that in his view
of things, there were no gods—oh, how
he wished there were!

He followed Sarkon down a rocky
path into a grove of trees where
the afternoon sun fell in splotches
on the ground. In the scarcity of
light he saw an old man sitting by
a rough wood shack. As he looked
upon the old man, he felt once more
the crumpled parchment in his pocket
and wondered if there would be ample
light to read it when the time
should come.

"My lord Sarkon," said the old man.

"Shhh! . . . " said Sarkon in reply.
"I've brought a visitor with me
today."

Everyman cupped his hand before his
mouth and whispered to his handsome
friend, "Why did he call you 'lord'?"

"He's an old fool," Sarkon answered.
And then he said, "Old Man, this is
a friend of mine . . . Let's not pretend
this afternoon. He wants to know if
you're the man who laid the Singer in
his grave?"

"I am, my lord Sarkon." The old man
turned his head away and fidgeted: He
had used the forbidden word again . . .
"Yes, I took him from the wreckage of
the great machine and buried him in a
rocky field not far from here."

"But," protested Everyman, "the
Singer's followers all say his body
was never found though all the wreckage

had been searched. In fact, they teach
he came alive again."

"They are liars," the old man said.
"I buried him and two weeks later
his grave was as I left it. He
still is there. Here's all of him
that I have left." The old man pulled
a broken lyre from beneath the crude
wood bench he sat on.

"Somehow I sense," objected Everyman,
"that you are right and all Singerians
are fools, but I can see so little
falseness in them. I think they
do believe they tell the truth."

"I tell you," argued the old man, "I
buried him and he is dead, and all
Singerians are liars and fools."
Each successive word expressed his
rising anger.

To Everyman the time seemed right to
pull the parchment from his pocket.
Sarkon shifted his weight from
one foot to the other as Everyman
read the strange words:
"In the name of Earthmaker,
Father-Spirit of the Singer,
be what you really are!"

They were strange words indeed to
Everyman, but no sooner had he
read them than the old man fell
forward on the broken instrument.
For a moment he lay silent on the
ground. Then an ugly reptile
lay in the old man's place. The

dragon hissed and moved toward
Everyman.

Bolt upright, Everyman stood stiff
and ceased to breathe.

Sarkon was silent, then he cleared
his throat and the dragon disappeared.

Everyman relaxed and regained
his composure, then asked, "Sarkon,
why did the old man call you 'lord'?"

"Come, Everyman. The taverns open
soon."

"No, Sarkon. I have seen what I
needed to see. The scrolls
have not allowed such things for
me. Yes . . . now I've hope. Your
monster set me free. For if the
dragons live, the gods may be.
Lust alone tonight, Sarkon.
I do not know if the Singer is alive,
but I do know this: Your old friend
never buried him."

Sarkon burned with anger as he
walked away. He took five steps,
stooped down, picked up a rock
and hurled it with more than
human force.

The sky swirled and the blood
ran warm across the face
of Everyman. He slumped to the
ground unconscious, and in his
great delirium were sweeter dreams
than he had ever dreamed before.

In the mist of his concussion swam
wondrous dragons and singers
in the streets.

Sarkon would have killed him
for the dreams if he had known
the nature of his sleep. But he
had other appetites to feed. There
were tavern maids and other youthful
scientists he labored to deceive.

XIV

I heard the ballad of a fool
whose simple song made synonyms
of life and death and cursed the
right and called it wrong:
    Come play along the precipice—
    Don't worry that the cliff is steep—
    The little flowers on the brink
    Are daisies, but their roots
      grow deep.

The Invader stirred within the drowsy
Anthem and he could not sleep. He
pulled his tunic on and then his
shoes and hurried out into the night.
His feet were given no instruction
by his mind and yet they fell in
firm intention. At last the meadow
hurried into trees and soon became
a grove so dense the starlight
halted on the tops of leaves.

He felt his way along in some
denial of the mission that he
could not comprehend, till in
a clearing where no star shade
fell, he saw a man lie wounded
in the night. He approached and
knelt in dust to lift the youthful
head which lay face down on the earth.

In a nearby stream he soaked his
shirt, then lifted up the head
and swabbed the dust and blood
away. It startled him to realize
the man in need was Everyman.

When he had swabbed the face the
second time, the youth awoke and
muttered from the mist that was his
mind. He sat upright and stared
into the night. When finally his
world merged with the one he sought
to see, he knew the hand that cooled
his brow was the singer that Sarkon
had stoned in his contempt. They
shared a common wound. At last words

broke the stillness of the woods.
Night silence surrendered up its hush.

"There are dragons!" said Everyman.

"Yes..."

"The old man did not put the Singer
in his grave!"

"No..."

"Why did you come?"

"The Invader led me to you
because the Singer loves you."

"Are the Singer and the Invader one?"

"As water and ice are one—or
heat and fire. The Singer came
to be a man, then came again
to be in man. The first time
that he came he was the Troubadour
and the next, the Wind Song."

"Why did the old man change himself
into a dragon?" asked Everyman.

"He did not."

"But I saw him do it here...
tonight... He changed himself
into a croaking evil thing."

"That's only as it seemed. It was
a dragon who had changed himself
into a man. The words you read
from the parchment scrap forced
him to become what he has been

through all time. A man can not
become a dragon. But a man may
sometimes be a dragon in disguise."

"But here tonight, he called
Sarkon his lord."

"Sarkon is his lord—he is the
lord of all dragons. And every
monster has the power of masquerade.
Sarkon himself loves the masque and
now he plays the role of mountain
god. The first time we met he was
a piper who played an evil song
to drive me mad."

"He was a piper then?"

"No more a piper than a mountain god.
He is his cloak, whatever garment suits
his evil purpose."

"And what is his purpose?"

"To smash the world the Father-Spirit
made and loves. He gloried in the
Singer's death and hates the very
thought that the Invader is the lover
of all men. He told you that there
were no gods?"

"Yes."

"He tells others that there are,
but he tells no one that Earthmaker
is the Father of the Troubadour."

"I dreamed in my delirium of dragons
bold and singers in the street. Tell
me of the song," said Everyman.

So Anthem sang in starlight the
Singer's story and when he came
to the Singer's cosmic moments
in the great machine, they both
fell on their knees.

"What must I do to be unchained?"
cried Everyman.

"Cry out your blindness and open
to the Wind."

And Everyman wept into the night
and sobbed his guilt:
"Earthmaker, I regret that your
Beloved died. I put away false
scholarship and pride. Come, Great
Invader! Move inside!"

Once more the radiance grew from the
stars till the Invader had buried them
in gusty hurricanes of brilliance.

And Everyman rejoiced to know the
living Singer who had smashed the
fetters of his intellect and let
his desperation out of hiding.

"I am unchained!" he almost shouted.

"You are indeed!" said Anthem.

"May I have the Stigmon?"

So in the raging light storm of
Invader's power Anthem drew a hand-
ful of the new earth. He traced the
Singer's Sign in the fiery luminescence
of Invader:
"It is only out of Terra's shame

That men of Terra wear the name
Of Singer,
Prince of Planets,
Troubadour of Life . . .
Earthmaker, Singer and Invader be
The substance of infinity."

Everyman surveyed the clot of earth
he held and rejoiced to see the stain
that symbolized the crushing pain
of the machine.

He stared into the glinting radiance
and repeated through half-opened lips:

"O man of Terra, fully know
There is no depth he would not go
To love."

XV

Yes, it was savage for the
rifleman to ask the weeping
mother which of her sons she
would like to have shot first.
But the greater cruelty is
to ask the frightened child
which of his parents he would
least prefer to live.

In the days that followed
Everyman and Anthem became
brothers in the spirit.
Everyman's deep resonance soon made
singing in the streets an eloquent
affair. Daily, as he finished the
Song, men and women, crying out to be
unchained, received the Stigmon.
Everyman offered it in the mystic
magnetism of his melody:

"It is only out of Terra's shame
That men of Terra wear the name
Of Singer,
Prince of Planets,
Troubadour of Life."

And he seemed to have a haunting
subtle light behind his eyes, while
the new earth fell from the hand
of the unchained:
"Earthmaker, Singer and Invader be
The substance of infinity."

But the grandest act of love for
the Singer was the Singer's Meal.
Everyman ate the crushed bread and
remembered the machine where the Prince
of Planets bled. He never tore the
wounded loaves but that he swallowed
hard in joy. Each time they met, they
took the Meal and said,

"And now the great reduction
    has begun:
Earthmaker and his Troubadour
    are one.

And here's the new redeeming
   melody—
The only song that can set Terra
   free.

The Shrine of Older Life
   must be laid by.
Mankind must see Earthmaker
   left the sky
And he is with us... They must
   believe the Song or die."

From day to day they sang the Star-Song
in the streets and ate the Singer's
Meal. In the homes and on the greens
they offered everyone the chance to
let the Great Invader into life. Those
who were unchained from month to month
received the Stigmon.

The days moved on and winter came
and then gave way to spring.
Both Everyman and Anthem went from
time to time into the Great Walled
City and sang the Ancient Star-Song
in the streets. They often saw young
Sarkon near taverns drinking ale with
students as he pointed fingers at the
pair and laughed. Once Sarkon even
sent a group of ruffians who seized
their instruments and harassed them
in the streets.

But not until the month of Krios
did destruction reach its apex.
It happened on a sunny afternoon
that an old woman entered the market
place near the spacious Plaza of
Humanity. She stood and spoke
above the gathering crowd.

"Men of Terra! Remember that our
joy is in the scroll of all the
ages. Our fathers loved this city."
She gestured to the gleaming
bastions of the Great Walled City
of the Ancient King. "But the
followers of the Singer say that men
must not love cities, for Earthmaker
does not hallow stone and mortar.
They cry against the songs the Grand
Musician sings before the shrine of
Older Life. They call our children to
despise our customs and our creed.
They say the recent rains have come
because the Great Invader came to end
the drought of desperation. They teach
that the Great Invader is the spirit
of their Singer whom we hanged upon
the battlements.

"They say the Singer lives and men
should turn aside our heritage and
follow him. They Lie! They Lie!"
she cried.

The crowd grew restless as she poured
contempt on all the Singer's followers,
who seemed to fill the highways and
the market places.

"I am the Keeper of the Scroll, yet
Anthem and the heretic called Everyman
tell everyone that I'm a croaking
dragon from the pit. They sing that
men must turn from me and follow
him who died and lives," she
screamed in fury.

"They tell our youth they must reject
the Scroll of Ancient Truth and follow

these young rebels who try to turn
poor Terra upside down with lies.

"They must be stopped. They are
vermin in the temple of our glorious
ancient truths.
Let vermin die
Or truth shall lie
Destroyed by our
Own apathy
Towards the Shrine
of Older Life.

"They must be driven out," she
rasped. "All who teach that
I am dead and thus to be despised
. . . Let's strike down Everyman
and his agnostic crowd, till all men
believe again that I do live and
hold the only scroll of truth."

Quickly Sarkon volunteered to lead
the group into the heresy-infested
ghettos of the city. As they moved
through the streets, many in the
angry crowd picked up stones.

"Where is Anthem?" said Sarkon to
a little singing group they
encountered in the streets.

"We know not, brother," answered
all the young Singerians.

"Do you believe the woman is alive
and that she owns the great brown
scroll of the only truth there is?"
Sarkon probed.

"No," replied a youth in simple

openness. He did not know the storm
his honesty was shortly to unleash.
"No, I don't... She died a year
ago before a village well. That
bent old woman is a dragon
from the pit."

"Blasphemy," croaked an old voice
in Sarkon's retinue. Sarkon grabbed
the young man by the throat and
screamed in red contempt,
"Infidel! You dare to call the
mother of our faith a dragon from
the pit?"

He struck the youth, who staggered
backwards with such force he fell
across an old Singerian who was
kneeling in the dust. They both
sprawled in the street.

"And you, old man. Do you believe
the Singer is alive?" Sarkon shouted
down in anger.

"I do!" the man replied before the
strong and brutish foot of Sarkon
fell with crushing force into his
abdomen. Sarkon kicked him
again full in the face. Blood
from his mouth coursed through
his silver beard. Unconsciousness
delivered him from pain.

In fury then the crowd that Sarkon
led fell on the group of singers
with clubs and stones. A little
girl who saw her mother bludgeoned
grasped her bosom just before
a flying stone in mercy made her sleep.

When the assailants had withdrawn, no
singers moved for most of them were still
unconscious in the street. Then some
began to stir, each reaching out to
others and offering strength and help.

Two never rose. The old man
hemorrhaged and died. The woman
who received the crushing blow
lingered till the night, then
peacefully she died. When her daughter
woke, she cried.

"Have you a father, little girl?"
an old Singerian asked. Her vacant
eyes said no. "I'll find someone
to care for you. Come with me
tonight," he said.

When word of the assault reached
Everyman and Anthem, the awful burden
of the Song began to settle on their
leaden hopes. The lamp burned low
while they groaned the pain that
seared their souls. They saw the ugly
storm they knew would come by day.
They ached in knowing those who
died were but the first. The Star-
Song stuck in their throats, and
nothing issued out except a lamentation:

"Oh, Father-Spirit, Father-Spirit:
Must truth be vanquished by the lie?
Must orphans watch their mothers die?
Must children whimper, old men sigh
And groan? Hear us for we cry!"

As they lifted up a crushed loaf of
bread to share the Singer's Meal,
light began to flood the table where

they sat. The Invader swept
throughout the darkened room till
every niche was born in brilliance.

Anthem and Everyman fell upon their
knees. Fire played upon the plaster
of the lamp-smudged wall and where it
danced, a vision grew. In the vision,
a behemoth red dragon, chained by his
great clawed feet, stood among such
temples as Anthem had not seen before.
But Everyman knew them well. Behind
the dragon, he could see the giant
gates of Urbis.

While they watched in horror, the beast
devoured a peasant. Then presently
the monster roared and leered
from Urbis into the very souls of
Everyman and Anthem. For a moment
the dragon looked like it would leave
the vision and walk into the little
room they kept. It leered from Urbis,
yet stared into their souls. Then
presently it froze, turned to stone,
toppled and lay dead.

Everyman and Anthem beheld themselves
beneath the dragon armed with bloody
swords. The vision fell away.

The Invader stirred warm inside
them, as the brilliance faded
till all the light was gone, except
for one small lamp that burned on
the table where they sat.

"Do you know the city that we saw?"
asked Anthem.

"Urbis!" said Everyman.

They knew that they must leave the
village near the Great Walled City
of the Ancient King.

Their destiny lay across the
Silver Sea in the city of the West.
Urbis, capital of Terra, a city
where the old woman and her scroll
had never been believed.
Urbis, the shining temple-city
of all the mountain gods.

They consorted with the leaders
of the Singerian Choirs and then
made ready for their voyage.

Months like foam flew by beneath the
keel. Krios came and went but not
their zeal. The Song thrived well in
salt breeze and halcyon seas.

60574

XVI

If Death and Life should ever wed,
There'd be no dynasty.
Their house would fall.

For Death would offer nothing
On his rigid firm demand
That Life must give up all.

The night hung close to the sea.
It seemed to Anthem that the sky
and sea so loved each other that they
merged and left no mark. Thus
often on the trip, Earthmaker and
his Singer merged into a single joy.

During the long voyage, Everyman
and Anthem sang while passengers
and sailors listened to the great
Singer's themes. Several in
the course of weeks cried out to
be unchained. One who sought but
would not yield was Praxis,
the Builder. He labored every
day on a great brown roll of
parchment on which he drew some
clean black lines of stress and
excavation.

"Tell me, Builder, what it is
that you draw," said Anthem.

"These are the plans for the great
temple soon to be built in upper
Urbis," Praxis then replied.

"Is Urbis short of temples?"
asked Everyman in disbelief.

"No. There are temples to all the
mountain gods but none to horses
ever have been built."

"Is yours to be the Temple to the
Horse?"

"Well... yes..." said Praxis.
"At least the unicorn..." Then
formalizing all his doubt he said
with certainty, "It will become the
Gilded Temple of the Unicorn. But
tell me of your Singer, and tell me
what it means to be unchained."

"You may only be unchained if you
renounce your petty dreams and
hunger to be free and come to life.
Then you will know the joy of
melodies that can swirl and echo like a
dervish in the soul," said Anthem.

"Must I give up the mountain gods
to know the Singer's music?"

"Yes."

"But why? Why isn't your Singer
the friend of all the other gods?"
thought Praxis half aloud. He thought
a moment and then continued as if he
had been overcome by a sudden trans-
formation of some lofty thought or
lost ideal. "Better yet, let's give
the Singer temple space in Urbis. I'll
save a handsome niche in the Temple of
the Unicorn where he may stand in state
for all the gods and ages to adore."

Anthem cringed. "No, Builder!...
He is not a mountain god,
for they are not. The Singer is."

"It's all the more a reason that
his reality cannot be threatened
by their non-reality. Let's bring
the Singer to the market place and

raise him in an arch of colonnades.
Let's lift him as a warrior king
in bronze and decorate him
as a slayer of the hosts. Can you
imagine how temple choirs could
sing the Ancient Star-Song in great
antiphonies? Thousands might call
out to be unchained."

He seemed about to cease his
rhapsodizing; then as an afterthought
he added, "He will need a consort
now, of course."

"A consort?" questioned Everyman.

"Yes, to keep him from too much
transcendence: It might destroy
him. Recall the myths. The great
gods never sleep alone or rule alone.
They live in pairs, and in their
heavenly sovereignty they need not
give up such delights as men can
understand. Men will not worship
long that which is too unlike them
or too far above them."

"But that's the meaning of the word
'unchained!' " protested Everyman.
"Freedom only comes when men give up
their grip on their humanity.
Mountain gods are made by men and are
too much men to help. They cannot
liberate who are not free."

The Builder took his pen and dipped
it in the ink and quickly drew a
sketch. It was the Singer as he
imagined him to look—a naked
titan whose great lyre hung

across his back. His heavy locks
of hair fell down over his ears
and sturdy jaws. His thighs were
marble pillars. The drawing was
an athlete god who bore a chilling
likeness to the youthful Sarkon.

He dipped his pen again. This
time he drew a lovely woman, supple-
breasted and yearning in idealism.

"Here," said the Builder, "is the
Singer and his mate. The simple
men of Urbis would worship such a
cosmic pair. Why in their fantasies
the two could romp through starry
constellations and their progeny
would be the infant galaxies. The
ecstasy that they might give the
poor of Terra would truly set men
free."

He stopped again while Anthem
shook his head. In flurried words
the Builder then erupted one
more time. "By the gods, dear Anthem,
we shall make him ride the unicorn.
Think of it! A strident warrior-
troubadour who reigns among the stars
with his great consort Radia. And
when they leave the unicorn to love,
the earth will yield great harvests
of fertility and joy."

"No, Builder!" cried Anthem. "Put
by your gods and unicorns. The Singer
is Earthmaker's only Son. He needs
no temple built by men. Temples
are prisons of both gods and men.

Stone redeemers neither live nor
come again."

"But," said the Builder, "let's edit
him and set him free. Not slay him,
just adapt his small ontology and
give him more humanity that we may
understand, that's all. Change
his solo to a choir and broaden his
small song till all the gods of Urbis
sing along."

Further argument with Praxis would be
to no avail. That both Anthem and
Everyman could see. The voyage soon
would end, and it was clear at least for
now the Singer's friends would not
include the Builder.

The Builder scooped his papers from
the bridge and walked away. The night
drew close; so therefore did the day.
Shortly after dawn, a sailor yelled
the sighting of their destiny. When
Anthem raised his head to look, great
golden Urbis floated on the sea.

Two left the ship to sing in
city streets that very morn. But
in one mind, the Singer sat astride
a unicorn.

XVII

Thank God the priests are dead
and stenographers type memos
where machine-gunned clerics bled.
We were surprised to hear that
the revolutionaries were atheists.
It should not have surprised us as
it did. We had forgotten that the
rabble teemed the lower city and
walked in rags and prayed to St.
Basil year by year. But the Saint
was far too busy with the Czars to
hear. It cost St. Basil everything
to be so uppity.

The Singerians were not so new to
Urbis as Anthem first had thought.
Some isolated groups of singers
were here and there in Urbis but
always in the lower city.

Lower Urbis was a tunneled plain
where lived the multitudes of
dispossessed. They were the secret
of the commerce of the upper city
where lived the Poet King and all
his complex court.

Anthem mingled in the tunnelways
of lower Urbis and listened to the
superstitions of the laundresses,
confectioners and old bootblacks
who labored there. They talked
in envy of the world above them,
the glistening city in the sun.

Some told of leopards near the throne.
Some thought the Poet King had
access to a gilded door that opened
on a magic flyway to the mountain
of the gods. Most in lower Urbis
did agree that the Poet King was mad.
Some said he was a cannibal who
glutted every night on the flesh
of infants kidnapped from the cradles
of the lower city. There were other
rumors more bizarre, but Anthem
listened long enough to know he'd
listened long enough.

Upper Urbis was a sea of great white
buildings that dazzled every visitor.

The temples and the senates and the
fountains were a sunlit demonstration
that those who lived in upper Urbis
were Terra's greatest souls.

Fear stalked both cities. Lower
Urbis feared upper Urbis for its
wealth and power. Upper Urbis
feared the tunnel dwellers
for the sheer weight of numbers.
Those in upper Urbis had their
dreams of horror, and in those dreams
the holes that led down to the lower
city swarmed with human insects
coming blind and powerful into
light—the vermin of the night
who lusted for the wealth above them.

Those who roamed the lower labyrinths
had long since given up their worship
of the mountain gods. The white temples
were the altars only for the cultured
and the rich. The upper-world elite
maintained the shrines, for they had
bread. The lower city worshiped only
bread and had no gods, nor wanted them.

Therefore when the Star-Song came
from eastern immigrants a year before,
it met the hapless lives of outcasts
in boroughs of the lower city. They
long had hungered for a god who could
stomach all their sunless miseries
and found such a deity in the Singer
and his Song.

Thus Everyman and Anthem sang
within the dripping caverns of
the underground, and multitudes
of lower Urbis were unchained.

Sometimes the knighted class above
would hear their songs coming full
and free from the passageways beneath.

Before a year had passed the Singerians
heard tales that in the East their
brothers paid for melodies in blood,
and it seemed that only time could
forestall the coming storm in Urbis,
too.

When the Singerian Festival of Life
was past and celebration slept, Anthem
saw a sign written in the language
of the West and posted near all
temples in the upper city.
   ATHEISM IS A CRIME
   PUNISHABLE BY DEATH.
He knew what theologians in the
upper city meant by atheism:
Atheism was disbelief in the
mountain gods. He feared the signs
the more because he knew that most of
his brothers in the boroughs could not
read them.

For a while the signs meant nothing.
The Singer's bands stayed clustered in
the tunnels where even the police of
upper Urbis feared to go. And the Song
passed from passageway to passageway
while seasons in the upper lands tumbled
over one another. More and more of the
tunnel dwellers cried to be unchained.

Each new Singerian received the Stigmon
in the dim light of lower Urbis. And
when the earth fell from their foreheads
and their hands, the words of the rite
echoed through the caverns:

"It is only out of Terra's shame
That men of Terra wear the name
Of Singer,
Prince of Planets,
Troubadour of Life . . .
Earthmaker, Singer and Invader be
The substance of infinity."

From day to day they shared
the Singer's Meal and celebrated his
death in the machine. The volume of
their singing grew until the Festival
of Life had come again.

The Festival of Life was the Singerian
holiday that marked the hallowed day
Earthmaker breathed into his executed
Son the breath of life. The Troubadour
was no longer Terra-bound. He had
come in pain to break the old and
obsolescent definitions of the dead.
The word "dead" was now taboo,
and those who were unchained considered
it obscene.

In the dancing and the singing of the
Festival of Life, a guardsman of the
Poet King had heard the joy and entered
the tunnels in disguise. Whatever
his intentions were, he found himself
compelled by great intrigue and the
Invader drew him into life. He fell
upon his knees and cried to be unchained.

In the weeks to come he sang discreetly
in the taverns and the halls of upper
Urbis and several in the very palace of
the Poet King became unchained. Their
atheism kept discretion and the Star-

Song moved in subtle circles of their
confidence.

Joy came to the upper city. Those
who knew the Song worshiped in the
labyrinthine covert ghettos
of the lower world. And more and more
they came, till the great Star-Song
was sung by many in the upper streets.

XVIII

Unicorns are garish horses void
   of browns and grays.
We let them live because we fear the
   humdrum in our days.

Look beneath the bloody beams of
   history and find
There is but one alternative to
   unicorns. The mind
May search for more in vain.

They are here," said Sarkon to the
Poet King of Urbis, "and they are
singing their strange songs against
the mountain gods. Yes, now they
sing in the upper and the lower
city and teach their strains of
atheism in the shadows of the
temples. Their teachings come encased
in catchy melodies that leave their
converts in a state of joy, and
crying out to be unchained."

"Unchained?" asked the King.
"Unchained from what?"

"From fidelity to mountain gods.
They left the East brief years ago, and
now they grow in heavy numbers here
in Urbis too. In the sunless tunnels
underneath us now they multiply like
rats in rotting earth."

Then Sarkon stopped and paced the
marbled flooring before he turned
in venom: "Not only that, O King,
but they insist their music is superior
to all the other poetry of Terra...
Yes... greater than your SONNETS
ON THE CITY or your immortal
EPIC OF THE GODS. They sing
in Terra's underground that no one
but the Singer and his Father are
to be adored and all the other
mountain gods must be despised. And
over all this blasphemy they teach...
I can barely speak their skepticism...

that you, O King, are but a man and
not a god at all."

Sarkon had lost no time in organizing
for resistance in the global capital.
In the few short months since his
arrival, he had brought the artisans
and scientists of Urbis to support the
traditions of the age. This was his
bold attempt to seek the audience and
power of Urbis' throne. He knew that
his performance must be polished and
convincing.

The King began to tremble slightly
as Sarkon spoke. Finally, he lifted
up his head and shook himself and
stood. At length he spoke.

"Is it true that Praxis, the sculptor
and builder, offered this strange Singer
a sacred niche in the Temple of
the Unicorn and his followers refused
the offer?"

"I too have heard it, and I think
it must be true," said Sarkon in
disgust. "I have heard their bold
Anthem will not let their followers
believe in unicorns at all."

"Not believe in unicorns!" cried a
nearby priest. He traced the sign
of Urbis in the air.

"It is true," said Praxis the Builder,
entering the conversation. "I offered
Anthem a temple niche for a statue
of their leader."

"But why did he refuse?" the King
asked in wonder and surprise.

"Because," replied the Builder, "he
believes there are no gods or unicorns,
and he does not want the men of Terra
to look on the Singer as another of
the mountain gods when they do not
exist."

"Enough!" cried the King of Urbis.
"The time has come to deal with this
blasphemous music loose among the
temples of the truth. Tomorrow I
shall have my knights set poison
to the lower city. And we shall
station soldiers at every tunnelway.
Those who survive will be clapped
in irons. We shall start the Games
of Karnos with the public execution
of all who refuse to confess the King
of Urbis to be god. Sarkon, you shall
be Public Prosecutor. You shall set
the penalty and nature of the punish-
ment for those who dare to disbelieve."

Sarkon, beaming at the King's response,
asked if the King could lead them in
the anthem to the mountain gods which
the Poet King himself had written years
before. The court of Urbis joined in
the music which the King led them to
sing:

"And when the wolf came down
    from the sky
And shook off the stars and left
    them to lie
In a pile of sparkling fire
    to be

The isle where Urbis took
    root in the sea.

And dragons came and took
    the land
And hissed their fire
    forbidding man
To settle in the dragons'
    lair,
The star-corpse isle that
    claws laid bare.

But the peasants prayed.
    Primeval morn
Then came on the horn
    of the unicorn
That pawed the sea and
    tore the land
And gored the dragons
    on the sand.

And where the blood flowed,
    there again
Would grow the souls
    of a thousand men.
A thousand gods were
    also born
On the giant horn of the
    unicorn."

While they sang the anthem, Sarkon,
who seemed the very incarnation of the
gods, walked out of the hall, pleased
at his new position in the service of
the Poet King. Praxis shortly followed
and soon caught up to him in the street.

"I'm almost finished with my statue
of the unicorn," the Builder said.
"As yet, the figure on his back is

still in uncut stone. I had offered
it to the Singer, but he will have
nothing now to do with mountain gods.
I wonder, Sarkon, if you might consent
to be my model for the rider of the
unicorn. Be mindful that it will
be years before his temple is complete,
but when it is you will be there,
timeless in the stone."

Sarkon agreed to be the model.
Praxis' chisel would leave him
for the generations yet unborn to see.
Sarkon loved his great deception.
The Singer's followers would die
for believing far too much. And those
who called them atheists would die
believing nothing much at all.
But he would play the temple game
with rare delight.

All who refused to kiss the
unicorn would die. The very thought
of Everyman and Anthem bowing at his
marble horse and crying out repentance
for their atheism filled him with
anticipation. He could barely wait
for morning when lower Urbis would
be poisoned. The lucky would die
swiftly in the vaulted fuming caverns.
The rest would live to be the sport
of those who loved the temples
and the bloody Games of Karnos.

"Do you believe in mountain gods?"
Sarkon asked the Builder.

"Of course not," answered Praxis.

"Nor I," responded Sarkon. "Isn't

this a glorious destiny? The labels
are so cleverly applied and misapplied.
All living is called death and truth
is called a lie by liars. Nothingness
affirms itself and substance is denied."

Before long they entered the sculptor's
studio. A great unfinished statue
stood before them.

"How long will this take, Builder?"
Sarkon questioned as he undressed to
sit upon a modeled framework of a
gallant steed. His brutal nakedness
led the Builder to applaud and trace
the sign of Urbis in the air.

"Six months I need to finish," said
the Builder, pointing to the statue.

"And will you promise me your soul
were I to give it to you in the
morning quite complete?"

"Impossible!" the Builder cried.
"But if you think it can be done . . .
well, yes. I'll give you anything
you ask."

"Very well. Leave me and you will
see me clearly in this clot of stone
come morning."

The Builder left and Sarkon gloated
once again that he was soon to claim
the souls of men who trusted both the
mountain gods and the Singer. But
best of all, he also owned the soul
of an artist who believed in neither

and therefore was most vulnerable
of all.

When the sculptor came early to his
studio the next day, he was stunned
by the finished statue. In flawless
polished marble his young friend Sarkon,
god-like and gallant, sat astride
the giant unicorn. Across his back hung
the lyre of the Singer—a divine riddle
in marble. Was he the Singer or
the Anti-Singer? Had he the power
of Earthmaker or the mountain gods
or neither?

The unicorn would bring life to
all those who kissed it in the
wisdom of denial. The unicorn gave
life therefore to traitors. The
rest would die and the dying would
come hard, for giant Tasman jackals
snarled in the pits where they
were kept.

Urbicide became the fashion of the day. Killing lower Urbis was accomplished by a dozen knights who entered the tunnels of the underground near noon. A torch was set on oil-soaked leaves of poisonous root moss, and the smouldering fumes swirled and eddied through the labyrinth. The caverns became death chambers where old Singerians died in rags and children breathed their final breath. Mothers clasped infants and fell across them to shield them from the evil haze. There was no place or time to sing the one great melody for which they lived . . . and died.

Only those within a few steps of outside air survived, and as they staggered to the fresh clean air of day, each was clamped in chains and taken to the prison yards to await their sentencing.

Everyman and Anthem were spared the poisonous caverns of the underground. They had gone early in the day to sing in the construction camps where tradesmen labored with the quarried stones to move them into columns of the city's latest temple. From every tunnel exit they heard the wailing of arrests. Lower Urbis died by nightfall.

Everyman and Anthem searched for someplace to wait the coming storm. They found a small forgotten park,

XIX

Urbicide may be as quick as a
coronary
Or as painful as the cancer ward.
Some cities die very fast:
Hiroshima, Pompeii, Sodom.
Some cities die very slow:
Masada, Sparta, Dresden.
Ask Leningrad (which took 900 days
to die) who was more blest.
They envied Nagasaki for her fireball
from the West.

grown up in weeds, that sheltered an old
grotto in decay. They prayed in silence
for their brothers in the tunnels.

The day was marked by such arrests
as Urbis had never seen before.
Singerians by hundreds were herded
into cells so gorged that there was no
room to lie or sit.

When morning came construction crews
arrived at every opening to the lower
city. The poisoned air was sealed in by
masons who built walls at every entrance.

A brokenhearted Anthem wept.
None who lived were sure who the
survivors were. Nightly as the
sun went down, grief-laden voices rose
from a hundred cells and the Star-Song
floated on the air:

"In the beginning was
    the song of love.
Alone in empty nothingness
    and space
It sang itself through
    vaulted halls above,
Reached gently out to
    touch the Father's face . . ."

Upper Urbis battened down their windows
to keep the music out, but still it
filtered through the lattices so that
the free men of the city wondered who
was really free. Only those unchained
could know.

The music of a free man taunts
a slave. And the free were found only

in prison cells and tunneled
tombs below. The rest of Urbis prayed
for freedom to the unicorn of life
and tried to sleep. But sleep, like
freedom, came only to the prisoners.

In the weeks that passed before the
Games of Karnos hope began
to circulate among the prison cells.
"The Singer will return and smash the
structures of the state. The Poet King
and Public Prosecutor will be swallowed
by the Canyon of the Damned." Thus
spoke the hope.

On the eighteenth day of the
imprisonment a baby died in cell
fifteen. The mother tried concealing
it but finally slipped it through the
rusted iron grate of her cell door.
She saw her baby moved along before
the shovels which pushed the human
residue into the drayage carts. The
mother cried to the Singerians in her
cell, who were again reminded
of the coming Singer and his promises
of victory.

On the twenty-second day of the
imprisonment a woman became sick in
cube eighteen. Her fever sparked
attempts at quarantines. Within a week
most of the cell was sick. The guards
themselves contracted the contagion and
the fever spread throughout the camp.
The death toll was most severe among
the very young.

The victims of disease were burned.
And so by day the prisoners could see

the smoke columns rise where bodies
burned outside the prison yards.

Seven days before the Games of Karnos
Everyman sent a small scroll wrapped
in a sheath of wax. He gave it to the
sentry with a bribe. The guard slipped
the scroll into a pail of swill and
passed it through the gate in cell sixteen.

A convert finding it, stripped all
the wax away. The scroll was dry.
Its title: THE FINALE!
Its subject: Hope!

"Death cannot be to those who know
The Troubadour of Life. He gives
A crown to every man who shows
By dying that the Singer lives.

So give the breath you cannot keep
To gain the life you cannot lose.
Before the Axman never weep,
But sing with Joy the Singer's truths.

The prince of dragons soon must fall
Before the Prince of Planets."

The scroll told futuristic tales the
prisoners could never fully understand.
Its saga brimmed with beasts and armies
and cities under siege. Most of them
rejoiced at paragraphs they understood.
Urbis, tyrant of Terra, was mentioned by
her ugly name. She would be destroyed
for all her sins, and the Poet King
and Prosecutor would be sentenced at
the throne of Earthmaker.

The scroll was passed from fevered hand

to fevered hand and the Singerians
sang a new hymn, one that spoke of
hope. Most felt the Singer would
return before the dreadful Games
began. And so they sang:

"He comes in power,
Rejoice the hour of
    jubilee is near.
Lift up the cry
Before we die,
    our Singer will appear."

Sarkon made the Builder his chief aide
to organize mass execution of all
Singerians. Three days before the
long-awaited Games were scheduled to
begin, the Public Prosecutor announced
a special mandate to the wardens of
the prisons: "All children in the cells
below the age of seven summers must
be taken from their parents."

This would test their victory and joy.
They lifted up their voices and begged
the Singer come.

XX

It's strange that Spartacus forgot
to tell his brothers in rebellion
that they would all be crucified.
When there are too many crosses
there are none.
A drop of blood is ghastly.
A sea of blood accepted.
We weep above a single dying beast
but whistle past a slaughterhouse.

You are my aide," said Sarkon
to the Builder. "You must be
the one to see the mandate is
carried out."

"But why?" asked Praxis.

"Because the children should be cared
for in a special way before their
parents die in the great stadium.
It hardly seems humane to throw them
to the beasts; they are so young."

"Oh, come now," the Builder then en-
joined with mock compassion. "Since
when have you become concerned about
the welfare of children?"

"There is a fear that if the beasts
in the arena seize and devour
a small child they may not even lunge
at those adults we wish destroyed."

"But what of mercy? Do we simply
tear them from their mothers' arms?"

"If they will not give them up in
peace," said Sarkon.

"Peace . . . peace . . . No . . .
I cannot do it."

"You will do it," Sarkon shouted in
growing rage. "I finished up your
unicorn in a night. You promised
me your soul. Have you forgotten,
Sculptor? I own you now."

"But the children?" he protested,
somewhat weaker than before. "The
little children?"

"They are the slime and filth of lower
Urbis. They do not trust in unicorns
or mountain gods. All such atheists
must die."

"But you do not believe in unicorns
or gods and yet you live," said Praxis.

"Nor you, Builder. But your unbelief
will make the job I give you easier.
Look at it this way: If there really
are no gods, there's no morality or
crime. And without gods, what
difference does it make? The children
you slay are a small function of flesh,
tiny claw and organ—a passing movement
in the sea of time. They are machines
which eat the general welfare. In
slaying them, therefore, you are a saint
who stops their pointless eating of the
common good. Yes, Praxis, drag them
from their mothers and do not spare
them for their screams. Here are your
orders for the prison wardens."

Praxis was ripped by shame, and burned
in furious hatred towards Sarkon, but
he took the scroll and left.
The children would be placed in the
chambers of a cave and poisoned in
the fumes of root moss.

Praxis trudged the heavy furlongs to
the prison yards in agony of soul—
a soul that he no longer owned. He had
decried all serious belief. Now he had

grave doubts about his doubts.

Once in the prison, he read the orders
from the scroll and shouted to the
crowds that huddled in the cells:
"Every child of less than seven summers
must be yielded up. You have the
promise of the state that they will die
most mercifully in the caverns of
Karnos."

A flood of agony swept through the
cells. There were no tears, just
stunning disbelief. Shock tore the
tongue of desperation from the hour
of doom. Mothers drew their little
ones tightly to themselves and stared
wide-eyed at the gratings of their
cells.

"Simply pass your children out the
door, as every door is opened, one
door at a time. Don't try escape or you
will die ahead of time, and your children
will not die in mercy but be clubbed
before your eyes."

Praxis hated his decree. And he hated
Sarkon. But more than all he hated
Praxis. He wished the Singer really
were alive and would come and strike
him dead and save them from this hour.

The door to cell one was opened
wide and two small forms were laid
outside—dead. There were red marks
on their necks. They had been quickly
strangled by their mothers. The muffled
sound of weeping blasphemed the
inner-sanctum of the prison. The soul

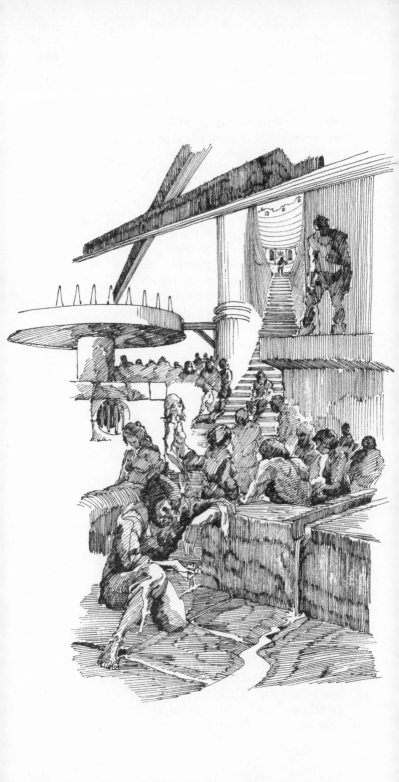

of Praxis now was gripped by high
compassion that would fold an infant
into gentle death before it laid a
frightened child before such lonely
dying as the executioners of Urbis
could supply.

In cell two a mother without the
strength to slay her son tried
desperately to hold him tight, until
a knight pulled the frightened child
away and bludgeoned his mother with
a mailed glove. He slammed the door
as she fell backward screaming. The
child beheld her mangled face with
terror in his own. Something in the
Builder died.

Praxis cried when cell three was
opened. Three of the children who were
placed outside were strangled. Two
more reached in horror for the parents
they would never see again.

Before the fourth cell opened, a
low and plaintive chorus had begun,
and song spilled into the courtyard,
flooding every cranny of the prison
with the chorus of their hymn of hope.
    "He comes in power,
     Rejoice the hour of
        jubilee is near."

All afternoon the work went on. Most
children laid outside were dead. The
dead were placed on one cart, the living
in a cage with high iron sides. Their
wailing played counterpoint to
the Singer's song of hope.

The crying and the joy filtered through
the souls of guardsmen, knights and
courtiers.

The inmates would have loved to have
the Singer's Meal, but they had no
bread. So as they joined in singing
once again the Star-Song, a radiance
garnered light from torches and
spread in brilliance through the
cells. They sang in brighter light
than any day.

XXI

We have heard that when the
commandant presided at the
execution of the first Jews, he
faltered momentarily. A woman
held up her infant to him, crying,
"Please take my baby." He turned
as though to spare her son the
rifle fire. And then he clicked his
heels and turned away. The next
six million souls were paperwork.
Occasionally he left the office with
a headache, but only because he
feared the gas was running low
or the cattle cars were late.

The unicorn was placed on a little elevation in the Stadium of Life the day the Games began. Hushed singing of the national hymn, the Anthem of the Unicorn, opened the festivities. Singerians were given their last chance to surrender their atheism and salute the great stone horse. Few did.

The events were divided into three separate games, each occupying about an hour. The first games were the Honor Games in which White Knights sought to defend their territory filled with atheists, while Black Knights tried to penetrate their lines and kill the rabble in the lime-chalked boundaries. The last White Knight with Singerians still alive was then declared the winner. Singerians not killed the first day became the victims of the next.

The second event was called the Truth Games. In games of Truth, knights of the unicorn advanced on foot to Singerians and offered them a final chance to recant and confess the true reality of mountain gods. One or two of those who huddled there did indeed recant. The rest were clubbed. The knight with the greatest number of "converts" was declared the winner. The "converts" were not many, but whenever a Singerian kissed the unicorn, a great cheer rose from thousands in the stands. Such Singerians were

spared and loaded into carts and sold
on auction blocks outside the stadium
when the Games were over for the day.

The third event was called Life Games.
In these contests, Singerians were
given a short sword and the right to
live until the morrow if they could
kill the giant Tasman jackals. These
beasts were set on them in pairs. Few
survived. Sarkon was pleased most with
these games which he himself invented
for amusement. He was always in the
stands, smiling over all the carnage
of the Games.

The Builder felt a strange revulsion
as he was seated in the Stadium of Life.
He refused to sing the Anthem of the
Unicorn and thought his protest went
unnoticed in the multitudes of those
around him in the stands.

The Games continued. Sarkon saw
the Builder leave the stands before
the main event. Misery dwelt in
the Builder's heart, and he wandered
as far away from the stadium as he
could. He finally stumbled on an
old grotto covered with vines and
broken beams. He entered in beneath
the shade of afternoon and sat down
silently. He buried his head in his
hands and tried to forget that he
was real. His soul, as much as
it existed, was under evil subjugation.
He wished, like mountain gods, that
he was not.

After several minutes he became aware

of men's voices praying and singing.
They were Singerians but somehow quite
familiar. Suddenly he realized that
Everyman and Anthem were in the grotto
too. In a moment the Singerians were
aware of him whom they had met
so long ago.

Anthem spoke in both surprise and fear.
"Peace, Sculptor! Are we now under
state arrest? We have heard, Praxis,
that you delight in murdering
helpless children."

"It is a lie! Sarkon owns me totally.
I never would have done it but for my
bargain. I traded him my soul for
the statue I wish I never had begun."

"Builder, would you even now be free
of such a bargain, if you could be
free?" asked Everyman.

"There is no hope. Earthmaker, if he
is, must loathe my wretched soul, if
I have one."

"Both Earthmaker and his Singer are.
And you may be unchained if you cry
out your guilt. Accept the Star-Song
and the Stigmon and join us in the
Singer's Meal."

In the distance they could hear the
muffled cheers of upper Urbis as
their brothers died.

"Hear the throng. They perish without
hope. Yet each believes the Singer
will return and rescue him from

death. I envy them even if he should
never come. Dying for any god is
better far than living without one."

"Oh, Praxis, cry out hope and be
unchained while there yet is hope,"
Anthem pleaded.

But Praxis turned and walked away.
He had been gone for just an hour when
Black Knights came to the gateway of
the grotto. Everyman and Anthem were
arrested. Sarkon, who had noticed Praxis
leave the stands, had sent some
knights to follow him. Thus the grotto
was discovered.

Sarkon was delighted at the capture
of the pair and told the Poet King
that the leaders of the Singerian
revolt at last were clapped in irons.

The public execution of Everyman was
scheduled immediately. Anthem was
placed in the cages for the Games.
But Everyman had been the special
grudge of Sarkon. Since he had given
up his science for the Singer, he
would die a special death.

XXII

The son of a hangman will
play with ropes and dream of the
day he will have a scaffold
of his own to tend. But let him
drink too deep of love and he
will only stroke the hemp
and cry that he is man.

Praxis trembled when Sarkon told
him he would be the executioner
of honor. His job was to set
the torch to the oiled faggots at
the feet of Everyman.

"Plague and Singerians must be handled
just alike or they will spread," Sarkon
said. "When he is bound upon the wood,
you only have to take the torch and
plunge it at his feet. Just think,
dear Praxis, you are the doctor of the
sick mentality that eats like cancer
on the great traditions of our state."

"I cannot do it!" cried Praxis.

"We have a bargain . . . I own the
soul you don't believe you have,"
said Sarkon. "And you will burn the
faithless flesh of Everyman—and the
unicorn will guard your way."

"There is no unicorn," groaned Praxis.

But they had been through all that
before. He suffered guilt until the
evening of the execution came. The
knights of Urbis delivered Everyman
and laid him on the wood. The rough
sticks cut into his abdomen and shoul-
ders. A priest of temple twenty-three
put the oil of mercy on his shoulders
to make his dying easier. Then in the
custom of his faith, he spat into the
face of Everyman and spoke the liturgy

of heresy. He rang three silver bells
and walked away.

A priest of temple seventeen led the
crowd of citizens in singing the Anthem
of the Unicorn. When the singing had
subsided, Praxis took the torch and
advanced to the naked unbeliever. As
Everyman and Praxis faced each other
it was clear which one of them was
desperate.

"Please believe in unicorns," the
Builder begged the youthful scholar.
"Believe and I'll not have to touch
this wood with fire. Believe in just
a few of the gods! Kiss the unicorn
and live! Think of me, Everyman! I
cannot live beneath the awful crime
you force me to commit."

"Come, know the Singer's love and
be unchained," said Everyman in
peace. "Yes, come and die
with me and you will know a life
that fire can never touch. You
don't belong to Sarkon. Cry out
to the Singer and you will be
unchained."

Tears glistened in the eyes of Praxis.
He hesitated. And then, instead of
touching the wood with fire, he hurled
the torch at Sarkon and fled into the
thickening gloom of dusk. The speed
with which he acted so surprised the
guards that they permitted him to
leave. Besides, they had no formal
warrant to arrest the master builder
of the state.

By the time that Sarkon picked the
torch and struck the flame, Praxis had
disappeared. Everyman stretched himself
upon the burning wood and died.

Praxis knew Sarkon would waste no time
in finding him. He ran until his
breath gave out, and then he rested
underneath a crannied arch. In tortured
desperation he looked up to the
evening sky.

"Father of the Singer," he implored,
"if you are there, I cry in guilt of
blood and death. In your great heart
can there be love enough to wash from
me the highest crimes of Terra? I
am a wretched, evil man," he sobbed in
violent convulsions. "Oh, Father-Spirit,
if you are, lay me on the wood.
Let Everyman go free."

"Everyman is free!" said a voice
behind him. He cringed to see it
was a White Knight.

"Are you here for my arrest?" asked
Praxis.

"No, I am a Singerian myself. I too
will shortly be arrested. And since I
serve in the King's Guard, I will be
shot by archers. But Everyman is free.
Sarkon only took from him the life no
man can keep to give him one no man
can lose."

"I hunger for the meaning of your
words. I too will die but only
for disobeying Sarkon."

"I saw you throw the torch and followed
you. Sarkon picked up the fire and set
it on the pile of wood, and Everyman
himself became a torch to light the
way to the courts of the Father
of the Singer. Sarkon is afraid.
Each time a Singerian dies in the
Stadium of Life two more leave the
stands. Sarkon fights a futile battle
and he knows it. Even now more than
thirty knights in the Guard of Urbis
believe."

"Don't you mean disbelieve?
Atheism is the charge for which
they die."

"No, Singerians are the true believers.
Don't you see that when they die there
is no emptiness of soul? Only they
are free who die in joy."

"Tell me, Knight, would the Singer
ever ask that children die in
caves?"

The knight, seeing the burden of Praxis'
guilt, asked, "Have you heard the
Star-Song yet?"

"Once when coming to this city
I listened while Everyman sang its
majesty of hope. Then it seemed a
pagan hymn. Now I do not know . . ."
His voice trailed off again.
"I remember just a few lines."

In a low voice the knight began to
sing the words Praxis first heard on
the open sea . . .

"His melody fell upward
    into joy
And climbed its way
    in spangled rhapsody.
Earthmaker's infant stars
    adored his boy,
And blazed his name through
    every galaxy.

'Love,' sang the Spirit Son
    and mountains came.
More melody, and life
    began to grow.
A song of light and darkness
    fled in shame
Before a universe
    in embryo."

The fullness and the quiet of majesty
began to settle on them both. The
Invader came in heavy presence to the
star-hung canopy of crumbled stone.
Mysterious light came gusting through
the ghetto.

As the final strains of the Song faded,
Praxis cried out to be unchained and
the scales of his reluctance fell away.
The awful burden of his crime was lifted
and the Invader, powerful and whole,
swirled light into the darkest fissures
of his soul. Praxis felt the buoyant
delirium of that great discovery that
indeed he had a soul.

"Please, Knight, grant to me the
Stigmon," he pled. The knight picked up
a bit of soil and traced the Singer's
Sign upon the sculptor's face. He
spoke the words of life so glorious

to those who were unchained . . .
"Earthmaker, Singer and Invader be
The substance of infinity."

He and the knight embraced and
parted in the joy he knew was
his forever. He stopped in the
dark street, threw back his head
and laughed a free man's laughter.
He shouted to the stars that had
absorbed Invader's outer light:
"I love you Singer, Prince of
Planets, Troubadour of Life."

And then, he paused and remembered
he was still a part of Urbis and
a servant of the Poet King—or was he?
He turned toward the temples of the
city and shouted fearlessly, "Sarkon,
wherever you are, your grasp of
death is over! I am a Singerian!
Yes, Yes!" he laughed and shouted.
"I, Praxis, am a Singerian!"

None had ever sung it quite so
loudly in the streets of upper Urbis.

XXIII

Creativity can sometimes be a curse.

Ask Dr. Frankenstein.

In half an hour Praxis approached
his studio. Two guards were waiting
at the door. One thing was left to
care for before he submitted to arrest,
and then of course to death.

As he had hoped, the back door was
unguarded. He slipped the key into
the lock and edged the door ajar.
The great leather hinges held their
peace and did not creak. Once in the
studio he felt his way from surface to
surface till his fingers felt
the head of his greatest hammer. He
lifted it in silence from its place
and stole away. The guards in front
were unaware that he had come and gone.

He hurried through the streets until
he came upon the causeway to the
Stadium of Life. The night patrols
recognized him but had not heard he
was a public enemy. Thinking him
the favored aide of the august
Public Prosecutor and Urbis' royal
sculptor, they let him pass. He wound
his way to the ramps that led to the
arena floor and there gilded in
moonlight stood the great statue that
he had made in one long year of toil.

He thought about the weeks it took
to shape the unicorn's great
lifted leg, then drew his hammer back
and heaved it in an arc of power.
The stone leg shattered into silver
shards ignited into sparks by moonlight.

He remembered how the great white
flanks had yielded in the passing
of the months to the urging of his
chisel. Now with brutality he swung
the hammer and a ton of stone came
crashing down. As the body of the
great horse fell, the head of Sarkon
struck the paving and rolled free.

The patrols rushed in when they
heard the raucous clatter of the
statue in disintegration. Praxis
raised his hammer once again and
brought it down on the severed head
of Sarkon. The god-like jaw split.
The heavy forehead shattered.

Praxis was arrested in the marble
wreckage of the unicorn. Even as
the guards held the sculptor fast,
he looked up at the empty stands.
The veins of his neck stood out.
He sang with power.

"And now the great reduction is begun:
Earthmaker and his Troubadour are one."

The stands of the great stadium were
silent in the starlight.

XXIV

The day of one's death is
a good day to be really alive.

T he sunlight was blinding as the
Life Games began. Anthem and Praxis
were the main event and thus released
to die at once. They issued under
guard from the darkened passageway that
led from underneath the lower stands.
The grate lifted and closed behind
them.

Blinking in the dazzling light, Anthem
saw the grinning Sarkon in the royal
box with the Poet King himself. But
Anthem had grown weary with the ancient
struggle. His mind went back to the
wall where first he met the World Hater,
now the gloating Sarkon, Public
Prosecutor. Not many years had gone,
but his eyes had beheld all the human
savagery that he could tolerate. The
letting of his own blood he knew to be
the grim necessity for opening
the last grand gate of life.

Anthem and Praxis advanced to the
center of the ring and knelt. The
grating on the west flew open and the
giant Tasman jackals leapt into the sun.

Urbis in the passing of the years
became the lair of wolverines. And
in the crawling centuries her temples
crumbled. Terra waited for her final
fate. In a day that none could know
the Singer triumphed and the mountain
gods were all forgotten.

But Sarkon lived and changed his

face and promises for every
generation. And centuries ran down
like wax into some lost abyss.

Then time threw orbit wires around
the planet Terra and silver-suited
men looked out through domes of glass.
And in the center of the universe
the Singer and his Father spoke of
final victory. The ancient World Hater
heard their whispered plans and trembled.

The Prince of Dragons gazed through
a thousand fields of stars, and
across the gleaming universe he saw
the Prince of Planets and steeled
himself for conflict. The light
of the Invader glinted from the
Singer's Sword. A great galactic
storm was gathering among the stars
and Terra lay directly in the wake.

THE SONG

a poetic narrative in the tradition of C. S. Lewis's Narnia Chronicles and J. R. R. Tolkien's Lord of the Rings trilogy—is Calvin Miller's sequel to his earlier, very popular book *The Singer*. In *The Song* Miller tells the story of Anthem and Everyman who leave the Great Walled City and travel to Urbis, the city of the Poet King, where followers of the Singer are martyred for their faith. As *The Singer* parallels the story of the Gospels, so *The Song* shows certain parallels to the book of Acts, and *The Finale* to the book of Revelation.

Calvin Miller is a graduate of Oklahoma Baptist University and holds the Doctor of Ministries degree from Midwestern Baptist Seminary. He is currently the pastor of a church in Omaha, Nebraska, and is also the author of *Once Upon a Tree, Poems of Protest and Faith, Sixteen Days on a Church Calendar, Burning Bushes and Moon Walks, A Thirst for Meaning, That Elusive Thing Called Joy, Transcendental Hesitation* and *A View from the Fields.*

The cover and interior illustrations are by Joe DeVelasco, a Chicago artist whose innovative work has appeared in many books and magazines.

The Song is set in 10 point Palatino roman and printed by the R. R. Donnelley and Sons Company, The Lakeside Press, Chicago, Illinois and Crawfordsville, Indiana. The cover is printed by Frank Prasil Graphics, Evanston, Illinois.